THE QUANTITATIVE SHIELD

A Field Manual for Micro-Electronics Export Risk Scoring

Turning the BIS "Red Flags" into a Weighted, Defensible, System-Enforced Score

---

The Transaction Risk Score (TRS) Framework

Entity Risk · Geographic & Route Risk · Product & End-Use Risk

James R. Ferry II, CCS, CES, CIT

Operational Compliance Series · First Edition

About This Manual

Publisher: Trade Underground Press.

Document owner: Trade Compliance / Export Controls.

Version: 1.0 · **Effective date:** July 2026 · **Review cycle:** Semi-annual (see Chapter 9).

Retention: All records generated under this framework are retained for a minimum of five years, in line with the recordkeeping requirements of the Export Administration Regulations (15 CFR Part 762).

First edition, 2026. ISBN 979-8-9971499-5-6 (paperback) · ISBN 979-8-9971499-6-3 (ebook).

Disclaimer

This manual describes an operational risk-scoring methodology. It is a decision-support framework, not legal advice and not a substitute for a licensed export-control determination. The weighting coefficients, scoring rubrics, and thresholds are a reasoned baseline heuristic — a starting point to be calibrated against each organization's own transaction history, product lines, and current regulatory guidance. Classification of any specific item, party, or transaction should be confirmed with qualified trade-compliance counsel and the relevant regulator before an export decision is made.

How to Use This Book

The manual is a story wrapped around a system. It opens and closes with a single real-world-style transaction — the kind of order that clears every automated check and still turns out to be a diversion attempt. Between those bookends sit ten chapters that build the framework from first principles: why qualitative "Red Flags" fail (Ch. 1), the mathematics of the Transaction Risk Score (Ch. 2), the three scoring pillars and their rubrics (Ch. 3–5), the action matrix that turns a score into a mandatory workflow (Ch. 6), how to hardcode it into an ERP (Ch. 7), how to build a tamper-evident audit trail (Ch. 8), how to keep the model calibrated (Ch. 9), and a full case-study walkthrough (Ch. 10). Analysts can read front to back; implementers can jump to the rubrics, code, and the quick-reference scorecard in the appendices.

Two boundaries, set at the outset. First, scope: this framework addresses dual-use exports under the Export Administration Regulations (EAR). ITAR-controlled defense articles operate under a separate regime — administered by the State Department's DDTC under the U.S. Munitions List, with no de minimis and its own licensing logic — and are out of scope here. Second, the code: the samples throughout are illustrative reference pseudocode meant to convey logic, not production-ready, security-hardened implementations. Treat them as a specification to build from, not to deploy as-is.

Contents

Prologue: The Order That Should Have Shipped

It was 4:50 p.m. on the last Friday of the quarter when order SO-2026-88421 dropped into the queue. Fifteen hundred high-performance field-programmable gate arrays. Six hundred and seventy-five thousand dollars, wired and cleared. Buyer: a tidy little trading company in Kuala Lumpur. Ship-to: a freight forwarder in Istanbul. Declared end-use: "educational drone kits for local schools."

Dana, the analyst on the desk, ran it through the screening software the way she had a thousand times. The buyer's name did not appear on the Entity List. The forwarder's address did not appear on any watchlist. The system printed a single word in green: CLEAR. One click and the warehouse would print a picking ticket. The order would be on a plane by Monday, and the quarter would close a little healthier.

But something itched. The company was less than a year old. Its website was a single vague page. The ship-to wasn't the buyer at all, but a freight forwarder. Educational drone kits do not usually require aerospace-grade programmable logic, and school districts do not usually route their purchases through a free-trade zone two thousand miles away. Every one of those observations was a classic BIS "Red Flag." And not one of them had a box to check, a number to enter, or a rule that could stop the order. Dana had a text field and a feeling, and the clock was running.

That is the gap this manual closes. Not the absence of warning signs — there were five of them on Dana's screen — but the absence of a reproducible way to weigh them, combine them into a single number, and let that number, not the calendar or the commission, decide what happens next. By the final chapter we return to SO-2026-88421 and run it through the framework properly. The order does not ship. This is the system that stops it.

Chapter 1 · The Strategic Compliance Gap

1.1 The Architecture of Interpretive Failure

Global export compliance has historically functioned as an interpretive discipline rather than a deterministic science. Regulatory bodies — most notably the Bureau of Industry and Security (BIS) within the U.S. Department of Commerce — provide international trade networks with extensive, text-heavy frameworks designed to safeguard national security. Chief among these tools are the standard "Red Flag" indicators associated with the Export Administration Regulations (EAR). They serve as an early-warning system, alerting market participants to suspicious transactional traits: a customer reluctant to provide end-use information, a shipping route that is circuitous or commercially illogical, or a corporate entity whose physical facilities do not match the technical nature of the goods ordered.

These frameworks share one critical structural limitation: they define the qualitative boundaries of risk without providing an operational, reproducible formula to execute them. They tell an analyst what to look for. They do not say how much each signal is worth, or what to do when three weak signals appear at once.

Qualitative approach: Text-heavy rule → Analyst interpretation → Subjective sign-off → Audit exposure

Quantitative approach: Risk data inputs → Weighted formula → Objective score → Defensible audit trail

For compliance operations embedded in the semiconductor, micro-electronics, and advanced-computing sectors, this gap between regulatory intent and operational execution is dangerous. When a high-value order arrives for a high-performance integrated circuit, an advanced digital signal processor, or a dual-use field-programmable gate array

(FPGA), frontline analysts cannot afford to work in a grey area. They are asked to weigh multifaceted geopolitical variables against text-based legal narratives, and to do it quickly.

Without a mathematical anchor, risk assessment becomes highly subjective. It shifts with the individual analyst's experience, with the organization's immediate commercial pressures, and with binary checkboxes that treat every risk variable as equal. That structural flaw exposes the enterprise to systematic compliance gaps and serious regulatory liability.

1.2 The Illusion of the Binary Checkbox

Most micro-electronics manufacturers and distributors rely on automated Denied Parties Screening (DPS) software as their primary line of defense. These suites perform a valuable but structurally simple function: they run fuzzy-matching algorithms against consolidated government watchlists — the BIS Entity List and Unverified List, and the OFAC Specially Designated Nationals (SDN) List, among others aggregated in the U.S. Consolidated Screening List. If a buyer's corporate name matches an entry, the transaction is flagged and stopped. If no match is found, the profile clears.

This binary architecture creates a false sense of security in corporate leadership. Illicit procurement networks, sovereign espionage entities, and rogue military actors rarely transact under their true, sanctioned names. They operate through layers of unlisted shell companies, third-party brokers, and front companies established for the specific purpose of defeating a name-match filter.

When a front company passes the watchlist check, the entire assessment burden shifts to the analyst, who must now weigh the transaction against the qualitative Red Flags:

- Is the customer's business model aligned with the advanced technical nature of the microchips ordered?
- Is the delivery address a shared, multi-tenant virtual office?
- Is the route moving the goods through a transshipment hub near a high-conflict or embargoed border?

Faced with a text-heavy list of warnings and a blank field in a CRM, the analyst is asked to make an interpretive judgment call. In a fast-moving environment where fulfillment speed is prized, this approach breaks down. Because there is no formal mechanism to weigh a physical-address anomaly against a product's technical capabilities, minor flags are routinely minimized, dismissed, or ignored.

1.3 The Flaw of Subjective Narratives

When a company relies on qualitative assessment, it documents due diligence through free-text fields written by individual analysts. An analyst might review an order, notice a small anomaly in the shipping destination, email the customer, receive a generic reassurance, and record: "Reviewed regional destination. Customer confirmed components are for civilian infrastructure. Risk appears acceptable. Proceeding with fulfillment."

From an enforcement perspective, that narrative offers poor protection. If the shipment is later diverted to an unauthorized foreign military end-user, investigators will audit the company's internal controls — and a collection of unstructured, highly variable paragraphs reveals exactly the inconsistency they are looking for. Three specific vulnerabilities follow from narrative-based compliance.

The problem of variable competency

A senior specialist with a decade in micro-electronics logistics will notice subtle anomalies a junior clerk will miss entirely. A qualitative framework has no built-in guardrail to raise a junior analyst's output to an enterprise standard; the quality of the review is only ever as good as the individual performing it.

The vulnerability to commercial pressure

When a multi-million-dollar order is held in the warehouse at quarter-end, the compliance team faces real pressure from sales and executive leadership. A qualitative system leaves room for negotiation and "reinterpretation" of the risk to favor revenue. Without an objective numerical threshold, the standard bends toward the deal.

The absence of a consistent audit trail

Regulators do not merely ask whether a company reviewed an order; they evaluate the integrity and consistency of the methodology used. A stack of ad-hoc text justifications demonstrates an erratic, individualized approach — the opposite of a systematic corporate policy.

1.4 The Dual-Use Micro-Electronics Dilemma

The case for a quantitative framework is driven by the technical reality of modern micro-electronics. Unlike conventional military equipment, which is identifiable by its physical form, advanced semiconductors are inherently dual-use. A high-speed analog-to-digital converter, a radiation-tolerant FPGA, or a high-throughput signal processor can sit equally inside a civilian medical imaging device or the guidance computer of a missile.

This ambiguity is deliberately exploited. Illicit networks order commercial off-the-shelf (COTS) or industrial-grade parts featuring wide temperature tolerances, radiation resistance, or high processing speeds, and declare a benign application — automotive automation, agricultural drones, a university lab. Because the hardware looks identical regardless of its final use, a program cannot rely on the product classification number (ECCN) alone to manage risk.

The product's technical threat profile must be evaluated in tandem with the buyer's corporate transparency and the vulnerabilities of the shipping route. Qualitative frameworks isolate these three vectors and force the analyst to view each through a separate lens. A quantitative framework treats them as interconnected variables in a single equation — capturing the compound risk that emerges precisely when a sensitive component is ordered by a new company using an unusual route.

1.5 Bridging the Gap: The Quantitative Shield

This manual replaces qualitative interpretation with a Weighted Transaction Risk Scoring Matrix. It converts the warnings issued by regulators into numeric values that drive automated, system-enforced workflows. Instead of asking an analyst to write an opinion, the framework requires grading three operational dimensions on a deterministic 1-to-5 scale.

Pillar 1 Entity Risk (ER) weight 0.40
Pillar 2 Geographic & Route Risk (GR) weight 0.35
Pillar 3 Product & End-Use Risk (PR) weight 0.25
→ Formula engine → Transaction Risk Score (TRS)

Multiplying each pillar grade by its calibrated weight (0.40, 0.35, 0.25) yields the Transaction Risk Score (TRS). That score maps directly to a mandatory workflow: an automatic low-risk release, an enhanced-due-diligence hold, or a hard block. The transition from narrative to number delivers four strategic advantages.

- **Operational consistency.** Every transaction — regardless of the analyst's identity, location, or tenure — is evaluated against the same model, removing individual bias from the process.
- **System-enforced controls.** The scoring thresholds are wired into the ERP and warehouse systems. When a transaction crosses a hold threshold, the system locks the

inventory and prevents the generation of shipping labels or customs clearances without an authorized override.

- **Commercial insulation.** When an order is flagged, the decision is the output of an objective corporate model, not a lone analyst's opinion that sales can lobby to reverse.
- **A strong regulatory defense.** If a transaction is scrutinized, the enterprise can present a structured, data-driven audit trail showing that every variable was evaluated, weighted, scored, and logged — clear evidence of a rigorous, proactive program.

One honest caveat, stated here so the rest of the book can be trusted: a scoring model does not abolish analyst judgment, it relocates it. The question shifts from the high-stakes, all-at-once "should we ship this?" to a narrower and more answerable one — "is this buyer a 3 or a 4?" That is a better place for judgment to live: bounded, documented, and reviewable. But it is still judgment, and keeping those grades consistent from one analyst to the next is its own discipline, addressed directly in Chapter 9.

The chapters that follow provide the mathematical definitions, scoring rubrics, and integration strategies required to deploy the framework across global compliance operations.

Chapter 2 · The Transaction Risk Score Formula

2.1 The Mathematical Imperative for Weighted Risk

To build an effective defense against illicit procurement of dual-use micro-electronics, an enterprise must stop evaluating risk factors in isolation. Traditional programs address risk sequentially: screen the customer, check the destination, review the export-control number. This siloed approach misses how risk compounds across vectors.

True risk is an emergent property of the intersection of those variables. A radiation-tolerant microprocessor sent directly to a defense contractor in a NATO-allied nation is a very different profile from the same part ordered by a months-old commercial entity routing cargo through a notorious transshipment hub. To capture that compounding, the model integrates the separate dimensions into a single metric: the Transaction Risk Score (TRS). Using a weighted average — rather than a simple sum or unweighted mean — recognizes that not all vectors are equal proxies for intent, and formalizes those priorities so compliance resources concentrate where they protect most.

2.2 Formal Equation and Bound Constraints

The operational core of the framework is a linear, weighted scoring equation. For any cross-border order:

$$\mathbf{TRS = (w_1 \cdot ER) + (w_2 \cdot GR) + (w_3 \cdot PR)}$$

ER — Entity Risk: the structural integrity, transparency, longevity, and legitimacy of the ultimate consignee or purchasing entity.

GR — Geographic & Route Risk: the geopolitical risk of the destination together with the vulnerabilities of the transit path, transshipment hubs, and freight forwarders.

PR — Product & End-Use Risk: the performance thresholds, dual-use capability, classification status, and application alignment of the specific component.

Three constraints keep the model consistent across the enterprise:

- **Input bounds.** Each pillar (ER, GR, PR) is scored on $1.0 \leq x \leq 5.0$, where 1.0 is minimal threat and 5.0 is an immediate red flag.
- **Weight bounds.** The weights are non-negative and sum to exactly 1.0 ($w_1 + w_2 + w_3 = 1.0$).
- **Output bounds.** Because the weights sum to 1.0 and inputs cap at 5.0, the TRS is mathematically bound to the same $1.0 \leq \text{TRS} \leq 5.0$ range — which lets engineers set firm system thresholds with no out-of-bounds behavior.
- **Single-pillar floors.** A weighted average can, on its own, dilute a strong signal beneath calmer ones — so it is bounded by two single-pillar floors. The High floor: any pillar scored 5 forces a minimum tier of High (hard stop). The Product floor: a Product pillar scored 4 — a CCL-listed item — forces a minimum tier of Medium (hold). Both apply regardless of the computed TRS. The average governs the ordinary and compound cases; the floors guarantee a single strong pillar can never be averaged away.

Why the floors are non-negotiable

Consider a buyer that shares a facility with an Entity-List party, or flatly refuses to provide an End-User Statement — an Entity score of 5 under the Chapter 3 rubric, which mandates suspension. If the route is clean and the product benign, the weighted score is (0.40 × 5) + (0.35 × 1) + (0.25 × 1) = 2.60: "Medium," releasable by a manager. That is the wrong answer, and not only logically. BIS's Know Your Customer guidance (Supplement No. 3 to Part 732) is explicit that a single unresolved red flag creates an affirmative duty to inquire, and that a company may not self-blind. A model that averages a lone 5 down into "Medium" manufactures the exact "we scored it and it cleared" posture that reads as negligence in an enforcement action — turning the shield into the exhibit. The High floor guarantees the model can never be quieter than its loudest pillar.

The same logic reaches one tier down, and for the Product pillar it is not optional. A part listed on the CCL under a specific ECCN scores PR = 4, whose rubric step is to determine the license requirement. Yet with a clean buyer and route the weighted score is (0.40 × 1) + (0.35 × 1) + (0.25 × 4) = 1.75 — "Low," a greenlight that would ship a potentially licensable item without ever making that determination. That is direct violation exposure, not a logical wrinkle. So the model floors it: a Product score of 4 forces a minimum tier of Medium, and names the exit condition for that hold. Where an ordinary Medium hold clears on a notarized End-User Statement and manager sign-off, a Product-floor hold is released only by a formal license determination from trade compliance — matching the rubric's own step of determining the license requirement, and guaranteeing that no listed item can auto-clear. The same floor is strongly recommended for Entity 4 (which mandates a signed End-User Statement) and Geographic 4 (which mandates a spatial evaluation); the strongest posture applies it to all three pillars. The principle is constant across both tiers: an aggregate score may raise concern, but it may never suppress it.

2.3 Calibration of the Weight Coefficients

The coefficients are not arbitrary. They encode a compliance philosophy calibrated to historical enforcement patterns and the corporate-accountability standards regulators expect. They are a baseline to be reviewed, not a constant of nature (see Chapter 9).

Pillar	Weight	Strategic rationale
Entity (w_1)	0.40	Who is buying the technology is the single most reliable proxy for transactional intent. Products can be redesigned and routes altered, but intent originates within the purchasing entity.
Geographic (w_2)	0.35	Where the goods are routed isolates the physical vulnerabilities of transit — transshipment loops and diversion corridors that strip a shipment of its original paper trail.
Product (w_3)	0.25	The intrinsic technical capability of the hardware and the plausibility of its declared application. Weighted lowest because a controlled part is only a risk in the wrong hands, on the wrong route.

Weighting Entity highest means that any anomaly in the buyer's profile — no historical footprint, an unverified warehouse, a hidden beneficial owner — heavily influences the final score. Even if the product is commercial-grade and the destination appears friendly, a suspicious entity score pulls the whole transaction toward enhanced review.

2.4 Why Weighted, and Not the Alternatives

The choice of a weighted linear average is deliberate. Two obvious alternatives each fail in an instructive way.

The unweighted mean dilutes critical signals

If every vector contributes equally, each carries roughly 0.333 of the score, and a cluster of moderate signals can average out to nothing. Consider a newly incorporated buyer with a thin footprint (ER = 3) routing through a transshipment hub (GR = 3) for an otherwise mundane part

(PR = 1) — two elevated signals and one benign, with no pillar high enough to trip a floor:

> **Unweighted: (3 + 3 + 1) / 3 = 2.33 → clears as Low Risk**
> **Weighted: (0.40·3) + (0.35·3) + (0.25·1) = 2.50 → Medium — review**

The unweighted mean lets two elevated signals be diluted by one benign vector and clears at 2.33. The weighted model concentrates on the riskier vectors — the buyer and the route — lifting the identical transaction to 2.50, just across the 2.5 line (Low is strictly below 2.5), and into enhanced due diligence. Same inputs, opposite outcomes. This is the compound case, with no single pillar strong enough to trip a floor, that the weighting exists to catch; the floors handle the single strong signals.

The multiplicative model is too volatile

Multiplying the pillars (ER · GR · PR) amplifies extremes but explodes the output range to 1–125, making stable corporate thresholds impossible. It also suffers zero-skew suppression: a single low pillar (say PR = 1) collapses an otherwise alarming ER = 5, GR = 4 transaction, hiding the very signals that matter.

The weighted linear average sits between these failure modes — no dilution, no volatility — producing a stable, defensible score that keeps day-to-day logistics moving. The design is also robust against a specific evasion: a buyer who deliberately understates the product grade to slip past a product-only filter.

> **Evasion attempt: ER = 4 (virtual-office buyer) + GR = 4 (transshipment near a sanctioned border) + PR = 2 (understated product)**
> **Product-only binary filter: passes — the part looks low-tier.**
> **Weighted TRS: (0.40·4) + (0.35·4) + (0.25·2) = 3.50 → Medium hold, flagged for review**

2.5 Comparative Summary

Model	Formula	Operational weakness
Unweighted mean	(ER + GR + PR) / 3	Dilutes entity alerts; lets high-risk buyers bypass checks behind benign product/route scores.
Multiplicative	ER · GR · PR	Range explodes to 1–125; zero-skew suppression hides real threats behind one low pillar.
Weighted average (adopted)	$(w_1 \cdot ER)+(w_2 \cdot GR)+(w_3 \cdot PR)$	Stable 1.0–5.0 range; preserves priority of the entity vector; defensible and predictable.

Chapter 3 · Pillar 1 — Entity Risk (ER)

3.1 The Strategic Centrality of the Customer Profile

Entity Risk focuses on the customer, purchasing broker, or ultimate consignee. Assessing it means moving past denied-parties screening to score the organization's operational presence, lifecycle duration, and structural legitimacy. Because who is buying is the strongest proxy for intent, this pillar carries the highest weight in the model.

Analysts must watch for shell companies designed to mask the true consignee. When an entity scores 3 or higher, the analyst is required to initiate independent cross-verification rather than accept the buyer's representations at face value.

3.2 Proliferation Risk Indicators

Certain structural traits recur across diversion cases: a corporate lifespan shorter than the technology it is buying is mature; a registered address that resolves to a multi-tenant virtual office rather than an industrial facility; a beneficial-ownership chain that terminates in proxy directors; and a stated line of business that has no plausible need for the ordered part. None is conclusive alone. The rubric exists to convert their combination into a single, defensible number.

3.3 Entity Risk Rubric and Verification Matrix

Score	Operational profile criteria	Required verification step
1	Established, publicly traded entity. Multi-year record, clear corporate registry and digital presence; verified beneficial ownership.	Verify SEC / global corporate-registration records.
2	Private small-to-mid enterprise. Stable history (>3 years), clear local licensing, transparent physical address.	Cross-reference physical footprint on local mapping platforms.

Scor e	Operational profile criteria	Required verification step
3	Newly incorporated (<2 years). Minimal digital footprint, generic web presence, or slight industry deviation.	Request detailed corporate profile and articles of incorporation.
4	Operates from a multi-tenant virtual office. Mismatch between registration address and warehouse/operations.	Mandate a strict end-user declaration signed by a corporate officer.
5	Shares a facility with an Entity-List party, or refuses to provide a valid End-User Statement (EUS).	Immediate suspension; auto-escalate to the Chief Compliance Officer.

3.4 Automation: Entity Validation Engine

To apply these rules consistently at high volume, the entity assessment can be automated. The following Python function computes the ER score from structural inputs and returns the mandatory protocol.

```
import datetime

def calculate_entity_risk(longevity_years, has_virtual_office,
                          matches_watchlist, has_eus_refusal,
                          digital_footprint_tier):
    """Return the Entity Risk (ER) score (1.0-5.0) and mandatory protocol."""
    # Absolute hard-stop conditions
    if matches_watchlist or has_eus_refusal:
        return 5.0, "CRITICAL: Hard stop. Suspend order. Escalate to CCO."
    if has_virtual_office:
        return 4.0, "HIGH: Systemic hold. Notarized EUS + full UBO audit."

    score = 1.0  # baseline
    if longevity_years < 2:
        score += 2.0
    elif longevity_years < 5:
        score += 1.0

    if digital_footprint_tier == "vague_or_none":
        score += 2.0
    elif digital_footprint_tier == "minor_deviation":
        score += 1.0

    final_er = max(1.0, min(4.0, score))
    if final_er <= 1.0:
        protocol = "LOW: Verify registry. Standard automated DPS screening."
    elif final_er <= 2.0:
        protocol = "STANDARD: Cross-reference physical facility via mapping."
    else:
        protocol = "ELEVATED: Hold order. Request signed EUS + corporate history."
    return final_er, protocol
```

Entity Validation Engine — hard-stop conditions are checked first, then structural signals accumulate into a bounded score.

Chapter 4 · Pillar 2 — Geographic & Route Risk (GR)

4.1 The Geography of Technology Diversion

Geographic & Route Risk measures the vulnerabilities of the physical transit path and the geopolitical reality of the final destination. A large share of unlawful technology transfers is completed not at origin or destination, but in the middle — through common international logistics hubs where a shipment can be stripped of its original manufacturer manifest and re-papered toward a restricted end-user.

4.2 The Mechanics of Logistical Obfuscation

Logistical obfuscation is a primary technique of illicit networks. A request to ship advanced microchips to a trading hub with no clear downstream commercial application is a major diversion indicator. The tells are consistent: a generic freight forwarder listed as the final delivery address; multiple intermediaries handling the cargo without commercial logic; and a second leg that quietly routes toward a sanctioned border. Analysts must track every step of the transit path, not merely the named destination country.

4.3 Geographic & Route Risk Rubric and Verification Matrix

Score	Geographic routing criteria	Required verification step
1	Direct end-to-end shipment to a Tier-1 friendly nation (e.g., NATO ally) with no intermediate hubs.	Validate direct bill-of-lading documents.
2	Shipment to a friendly nation with standard, logical layovers and transparent customs controls.	Audit intermediate line-haul route schedules.
3	Routes via a known transshipment hub (e.g., UAE, Singapore, Turkey) using a generic freight forwarder.	Demand comprehensive forwarder ultimate-delivery proofs.
4	Final destination shares an active land	Perform advanced spatial and

Score	Geographic routing criteria	Required verification step
	border with a heavily embargoed, sanctioned, or high-conflict territory.	regional threat evaluation.
5	Highly circuitous or commercially illogical routing; multiple unverified forwarders handle the cargo.	Immediate physical hold; full supply-chain route audit.

4.4 Automation: Logistics Routing Assessor

```
def calculate_geographic_risk(destination_tier, uses_generic_forwarder,
                               borders_sanctioned_state, circuitous_routing):
    """Return the Geographic & Route Risk (GR) score and protocol."""
    if circuitous_routing:
        return 5.0, "CRITICAL: Physical hold. Full supply-chain route audit."
    if borders_sanctioned_state:
        return 4.0, "HIGH: Spatial/regional threat evaluation before release."

    score = float(destination_tier)  # 1 = Tier-1 ally ... higher = riskier
    if uses_generic_forwarder:
        score += 1.0


    final_gr = max(1.0, min(3.0, score))
    protocol = ("LOW: Validate bill of lading." if final_gr <= 1.0
            else "STANDARD: Audit route schedules." if final_gr <= 2.0
            else "ELEVATED: Demand forwarder ultimate-delivery proofs.")
    return final_gr, protocol
```

Logistics Routing Assessor — circuitous routing and sanctioned-border proximity are treated as hard escalations.

Chapter 5 · Pillar 3 — Product & End-Use Risk (PR)

5.1 The Dual-Use Nature of Advanced Silicon

Product Risk focuses on the intrinsic technical capability of the component and the likelihood it can be adapted for defense, aerospace, guidance, or electronic-warfare systems. The core diligence question is alignment: does the declared end-use match what the hardware can actually do? When a customer orders high-specification parts but describes an application that only needs low-tier commercial components, that divergence must trigger escalation.

5.2 Regulatory Framework: EAR99 vs. the CCL

Two classification anchors bound this pillar. At the low end sit EAR99 items — commercial goods not listed on the Commerce Control List, generally shippable without a license to most destinations. At the high end sit items enumerated on the Commerce Control List (CCL) under a specific Export Control Classification Number (ECCN), which may require a license depending on destination and end-user. Between them lies the dangerous middle: dual-use parts whose parameters (temperature tolerance, radiation hardening, clock speed, reprogrammable logic) push past ordinary commercial thresholds under a vague "R&D" justification.

5.3 A Note on Advanced-Computing Controls

The legacy integrated-circuit classifications — the 3A001 line and its neighbors — are no longer the whole story for high-performance silicon. Beginning in October 2022 and tightened repeatedly since, BIS built a dedicated advanced-computing regime around ECCNs such as 3A090 and 4A090, with controls keyed to performance thresholds (processing power, interconnect bandwidth) and to specific destination country groups. For high-end FPGAs, GPUs, and AI-class accelerators, this newer regime — not the older 3A001 entries — is now the center of gravity, and it frequently sweeps in parts a buyer will describe as ordinary commercial hardware.

Two implications for scoring. First, a Product assessment for cutting-edge compute must check the 3A090 / 4A090 family and the current destination-based rules, not just the classic control-list entries. Second — and this is why the rubric points to verification rather than fixed numbers — these thresholds and country groups change often. Any specific parameter cited in this book or in training material must be re-verified against the operative regulation at the time of the transaction; a value that was correct last quarter may not be this one. Where this manual names a specific ECCN, treat it as illustrative, not as a live classification.

5.4 Product & End-Use Risk Rubric and Verification Matrix

Score	Technical / end-use risk profile	Required verification step
1	Low-grade commercial off-the-shelf (COTS) item. Standard consumer-electronics or appliance use.	Verify EAR99 categorization status.
2	Industrial-grade component with expanded tolerances. Broad commercial use (e.g., industrial automation).	Cross-reference technical data sheets.
3	Dual-use component exceeding standard thresholds (wide temperature tolerance, advanced FPGAs). Vague "R&D" use.	Audit specifications against the Commerce Control List.
4	Item listed on the CCL under an explicit ECCN that may require a license for the destination.	Determine applicable license requirements or exceptions.
5	Military-grade or radiation-hardened part; stated application is inconsistent with the buyer's capabilities.	Hard stop; initiate comprehensive technical end-use review.

5.5 Automation: Technical Capability Assessor

```
def calculate_product_risk(classification, exceeds_commercial_thresholds,
                           end_use_mismatch, is_mil_or_rad_hardened):
    """Return the Product & End-Use Risk (PR) score and protocol."""
    if is_mil_or_rad_hardened and end_use_mismatch:
        return 5.0, "CRITICAL: Hard stop. Comprehensive end-use review."
    if classification == "CCL_ECCN":
        return 4.0, "HIGH: Determine license requirement for destination."

    score = 1.0
    if exceeds_commercial_thresholds:
        score += 2.0
    if end_use_mismatch:
        score += 1.0

    final_pr = max(1.0, min(3.0, score))
    protocol = ("LOW: Verify EAR99 status." if final_pr <= 1.0
                else "STANDARD: Cross-reference data sheets." if final_pr <= 2.0
                else "ELEVATED: Audit specs against the CCL.")
    return final_pr, protocol
```

Technical Capability Assessor — a listed ECCN or a military/rad-hardened part with a mismatched end-use forces the top tiers.

Chapter 6 · The Operational Risk Matrix & Action Protocols

6.1 From Analysis to Enforcement

Calculating the TRS is only half the work. For the framework to function as a defensive shield, the score must trigger a mandatory, standardized workflow. The action matrix binds each scoring band to a specific corporate response, so that a high-risk transaction cannot be released by an account manager or a logistics coordinator under deadline pressure.

6.2 The Three-Tier Action Matrix

The bands are contiguous by design — every possible TRS between 1.00 and 5.00 lands in exactly one tier, with no undefined gaps at the boundaries.

TRS range	Risk tier	Mandatory operational protocol
1.00 - 2.49	Low	Greenlight. Process through standard automated Denied Parties Screening. Archive the TRS and pillar scores automatically in the ERP.
2.50 - 3.89	Medium	Enhanced Due Diligence (EDD). Place a systemic hold. Require a signed, notarized End-User Statement. Verify facility coordinates via satellite imagery. Manager sign-off required. A hold triggered by a CCL-listed Product score (PR = 4) routes specifically to a formal license determination by trade compliance before release.
3.90 - 5.00	High	Hard stop / escalate. Block all automated shipping. Route the complete transaction file to specialized legal counsel for a formal license determination or rejection. File an internal suspicious-order report.

Note the two-stage lock: a Medium score triggers a systemic hold that can be resolved through enhanced diligence and manager sign-off; a High score triggers a hard block that no account manager can override — only a documented legal review can release or reject it.

The floors above the table

Two rules sit above the matrix; their full rationale is set out in Chapter 2.2. Any single pillar scored 5 forces a minimum tier of High, and a Product pillar scored 4 — a CCL-listed item — forces a minimum tier of Medium, regardless of what the weighted TRS computes to. A lone strong signal is a stop condition in its own right, and the aggregate may raise a transaction's tier but never lower it below what a single pillar demands. The weighted score decides the ordinary and compound cases; the floors guarantee the model can never clear a transaction its own rubric says must halt.

6.3 Automation: The Compliance Control Layer

```
def evaluate_transaction(er, gr, pr, weights=(0.40, 0.35, 0.25)):
    """Compute the TRS and map it to the mandatory action protocol."""
    w1, w2, w3 = weights
    assert abs((w1 + w2 + w3) - 1.0) < 1e-9, "Weights must sum to 1.0"
    trs = round(w1 * er + w2 * gr + w3 * pr, 2)

    # The weighted score sets the baseline tier ...
    if trs < 2.5:
        tier, action = "LOW", "GREENLIGHT: automated screening; archive score."
    elif trs < 3.9:
        tier, action = "MEDIUM", "EDD HOLD: notarized EUS; manager sign-off."
    else:
        tier, action = "HIGH", "HARD STOP: block shipping; route to legal."

    # ... but a single strong pillar can only raise the tier, never lower it.
    if max(er, gr, pr) >= 5:
        tier, action = "HIGH", "HARD STOP (High floor): a pillar = 5."
    elif pr >= 4 and tier == "LOW":
        # Product floor: a CCL-listed item (PR = 4) can never auto-clear.
        tier, action = "MEDIUM", "EDD HOLD (Product floor): PR = 4 needs a license
determination."
    # Recommended: extend the >= 4 floor to er and gr as well.

    return {"trs": trs, "tier": tier, "action": action,
            "audit_trail": "WRITE_IMMUTABLE_LOG"}
```

The weighted bands set the baseline; the floors below guarantee a single 5 lands at a hard stop and a CCL-listed part (PR = 4) can never auto-clear.

6.4 The Framework Also Says Yes

It would be easy to read this chapter as a machine that only refuses — and the sales floor's fear that compliance is a wall of "no" is worth disarming directly. Most orders are ordinary, and the model clears them faster and more consistently than a person deliberating over a blank text field.

A long-standing industrial customer reorders a mid-grade sensor component. Established private firm, transparent address (ER = 2). Direct shipment to its plant in a NATO-ally country (GR = 1). An EAR99 part it has bought a dozen times before (PR = 1).

TRS = (0.40 × 2) + (0.35 × 1) + (0.25 × 1) = 0.80 + 0.35 + 0.25 = 1.40 → Low

No pillar anywhere near a floor, a score of 1.40, and the order clears through standard screening — evaluated, scored, logged, and on its way in twenty minutes. That is the point of the model as much as the block is: spend scrutiny where the risk actually lives, and get out of the way where it does not. A framework that only ever says no gets switched off; one that says yes quickly and no firmly gets trusted.

Chapter 7 · Operationalizing the Math: ERP Integration

7.1 The Vulnerability of Human Intervention

For a scoring framework to work in a high-volume environment, it must be embedded in the transactional layer of the ERP — not left to a manual side-process that is prone to delay, inconsistency, and record gaps. When an order arrives via a sales portal or electronic data interchange (EDI), the ERP should parse the customer record, destination, and part numbers, prompt the analyst with the calibrated rubrics, accept the three pillar scores, and evaluate the formula instantly.

7.2 Hardcoded Database Controls

The most robust control lives at the schema level, in a database trigger that fires before the order row is committed. Because it runs inside the transaction, no application bug or user shortcut can bypass it. If the resulting score crosses the hold threshold, the trigger flips a lock flag that prevents the warehouse system from generating picking tickets, packing slips, or shipping labels until the required documents are attached.

7.3 Reference Implementation (PostgreSQL / PL/pgSQL)

```
CREATE OR REPLACE FUNCTION enforce_trs_scoring()
RETURNS TRIGGER AS $$
DECLARE
   v_trs NUMERIC(3,2);
BEGIN
   v_trs := ROUND( (0.40 * NEW.entity_risk)
             + (0.35 * NEW.geographic_risk)
             + (0.25 * NEW.product_risk), 2 );
   NEW.transaction_risk_score := v_trs;


   -- High floor: any single pillar = 5 forces a hard stop,
   -- regardless of the weighted score.
   IF GREATEST(NEW.entity_risk, NEW.geographic_risk, NEW.product_risk) >= 5 THEN
      NEW.order_state := 'CRITICAL_BLOCK_LEGAL';
      NEW.compliance_lock_active := TRUE;
   ELSIF v_trs >= 3.9 THEN
```

```
        NEW.order_state := 'CRITICAL_BLOCK_LEGAL';
        NEW.compliance_lock_active := TRUE;
    ELSIF v_trs >= 2.5 THEN
        NEW.order_state := 'EDD_HOLD';
        NEW.compliance_lock_active := TRUE;
    ELSIF NEW.product_risk >= 4 THEN
        -- Product floor: a CCL-listed item (PR = 4) can never auto-clear.
        NEW.order_state := 'EDD_HOLD';
        NEW.compliance_lock_active := TRUE;
    ELSE
        NEW.order_state := 'CLEARED';
        NEW.compliance_lock_active := FALSE;
    END IF;

    INSERT INTO compliance_audit_log (
        order_id, entity_risk, geographic_risk, product_risk,
        transaction_risk_score, order_state, evaluated_at, evaluated_by)
    VALUES (
        NEW.order_id, NEW.entity_risk, NEW.geographic_risk, NEW.product_risk,
        v_trs, NEW.order_state, NOW(), NEW.analyst_id);

    RETURN NEW;
END;
$$ LANGUAGE plpgsql;

CREATE TRIGGER sales_order_compliance_screening
BEFORE INSERT OR UPDATE ON sales_order_table
FOR EACH ROW EXECUTE FUNCTION enforce_trs_scoring();
```

A BEFORE INSERT/UPDATE trigger scores every order and writes an audit-log row in the same transaction, so a lock cannot be silently skipped.

7.4 Authorization and Digital Signatures

Releasing a held order must require more than a text password. High-tier overrides should demand a cryptographic digital signature bound to a named, authorized officer, with the signing identity and timestamp written into the audit record. The control is only as strong as the difficulty of forging the release.

Chapter 8 · Building a Defensible Audit Trail

8.1 The Paradigm of Regulatory Proof

In export enforcement, the primary measure of a program's efficacy is the audit trail. If a regulator investigates a transaction later diverted to an unauthorized end-user, the company must demonstrate an organized record of systematic due diligence completed before the goods left the dock. The TRS framework produces exactly that record, automatically.

8.2 Anatomy of a Defensible Log File

Every transaction — regardless of tier — must generate a log entry that permanently stores the three individual pillar scores, the final TRS, the evaluation timestamp, the identity of the processing analyst, and the justifications or source documents supporting each score. A cleared order is as important to log as a blocked one: consistency across the whole population is what proves the program was applied uniformly, not selectively.

8.3 Tamper-Evident, Append-Only Ledger

To withstand scrutiny, the log should be append-only and tamper-evident. Chain-hashing achieves this: each record stores a SHA-256 hash computed over its own contents plus the hash of the previous record. Any later alteration of a historic row breaks the chain from that point forward, making silent edits detectable.

```
CREATE OR REPLACE FUNCTION append_audit_ledger()
RETURNS TRIGGER AS $$
DECLARE
   prev_hash TEXT;
BEGIN
   SELECT current_row_hash INTO prev_hash
   FROM   compliance_vault.immutable_audit_ledger
   ORDER  BY ledger_version DESC
   LIMIT  1;
```

```
    NEW.previous_row_hash := COALESCE(prev_hash, 'GENESIS');
    NEW.current_row_hash  := encode(
      digest(NEW.previous_row_hash
          || NEW.order_id
          || NEW.transaction_risk_score::text
          || NEW.evaluated_at::text, 'sha256'), 'hex');
    RETURN NEW;
END;
$$ LANGUAGE plpgsql;
```

Chain-hashing: each ledger row is cryptographically linked to its predecessor, so tampering is detectable rather than merely discouraged.

8.4 Presenting to Regulators

When an auditor arrives, the goal is to show not a single decision but a disciplined, repeatable methodology applied across the entire transaction population. A serialized package — the score, the supporting documents, the signatures, the unbroken hash chain — demonstrates that the enterprise did not turn a blind eye, but applied its internal controls and made a structured, documented decision on the best data available at the time of export.

Chapter 9 · Continuous Calibration & Weight Adjustment

9.1 The Dynamic Threat Landscape

Geopolitical risk is fluid. A routing corridor considered secure today can become a diversion channel tomorrow through shifting alliances, changes in local customs enforcement, or the emergence of new front companies. The weights ($w_1 = 0.40$, $w_2 = 0.35$, $w_3 = 0.25$) must therefore be treated as tunable parameters, not fixed constants.

9.2 The Internal Compliance Committee

An Internal Compliance Committee should conduct a formal calibration review on a semi-annual basis, integrating recent audit findings, updated regulatory guidance, and macro-level intelligence. The review asks a simple question: are the weights still pointed at where the threat actually is?

9.3 Shifting the Weight Matrix

Suppose enforcement data shows illicit networks moving away from complex corporate structures and toward exploitation of freight-forwarding routes in neutral territories. The committee might reduce the Entity weight and raise the Geographic weight — for example, from (0.40, 0.35, 0.25) to (0.30, 0.45, 0.25) — provided the three still sum to 1.0. Every change is versioned and logged, so any historic score can be reproduced against the weights in force at the time.

9.4 Enforcing Weight Integrity in Code

The one invariant that must never break is that the weights sum to exactly 1.0; otherwise the TRS leaves its bounded 1.0–5.0 range. A database constraint enforces this at the point of configuration.

```
CREATE OR REPLACE FUNCTION enforce_weight_unity()
RETURNS TRIGGER AS $$
BEGIN
   IF ROUND(NEW.w_entity + NEW.w_geographic + NEW.w_product, 4) <> 1.0 THEN
      RAISE EXCEPTION 'Weight coefficients must sum to exactly 1.0';
   END IF;
   RETURN NEW;
END;
$$ LANGUAGE plpgsql;

CREATE TRIGGER enforce_weight_unity_trigger
BEFORE INSERT OR UPDATE ON compliance_vault.scoring_parameter_registry
FOR EACH ROW EXECUTE FUNCTION enforce_weight_unity();
```

A recalibration that does not sum to 1.0 is rejected at the database level before it can corrupt live scoring.

9.5 Keeping the Grades Consistent Across Analysts

The framework relocates judgment from "should we ship?" to "is this pillar a 3 or a 4?" — a narrower question, but still a human one. The weights are meaningless if two analysts grade the same order differently, so grading consistency is a control in its own right, not an afterthought. Three practices hold it together.

- **Rubric anchoring.** Analysts score against the written criteria in Chapters 3–5, not against instinct. Each score cites the specific rubric row and the evidence that satisfies it, so a grade is a documented finding rather than an impression.
- **Dual review on boundary scores.** Any grade that sits on a tier boundary — the line between clear and hold, or hold and block — requires a second reviewer to concur before the order proceeds. Disagreement escalates rather than defaulting to the more permissive score.
- **Periodic inter-rater calibration.** On the same semi-annual cycle as the weight review, the team re-scores a shared set of past orders blind and compares results. Divergence points to a rubric row whose language needs sharpening, and the exercise itself is logged as part of the calibration record.

None of this makes the grading mechanical. It makes it consistent, auditable, and improvable — which is the honest most a scoring model can claim, and considerably more than a free-text field delivers.

Chapter 10 · Case Study: Anatomy of a Blocked Procurement

10.1 The Inbound Transaction

Order SO-2026-88421 · 2026-07-16 09:14 UTC
Item: 1,500 × UltraScale+ FPGA (ECCN 3A001.a.7.c) · Value: $675,000
Buyer: Nusantara Aero-Tech Logistics, Kuala Lumpur
Ship via: Apex Forwarding, Istanbul free-trade zone, Turkey
Declared end-use: "Educational drone-kit assembly for local schools"

Under legacy procedure, this order would have generated a Denied Parties screen, matched nothing, printed "Clear," and gone to the warehouse floor. Because the enterprise hardcoded the TRS framework into its database triggers, the transaction took a different path: the moment the EDI insert reached the sales-order table, the trigger paused the write and launched the scoring routine.

10.2 Scoring the Three Pillars

Entity Risk

A corporate-registry query showed the buyer had been incorporated 11 months before the order (<2 years). Geospatial checks resolved its headquarters not to an industrial facility but to a multi-tenant virtual suite in a Kuala Lumpur commercial tower. Its digital footprint was a single-page template on a proxy domain describing "global technology sourcing." Against the Chapter 3 rubric, this is an opaque entity in a virtual office with an unverified footprint: ER = 4.0.

Geographic & Route Risk

The cargo was to ship from Southeast Asia to Apex Forwarding, a small independent broker in an Istanbul free-trade zone, with no internal compliance systems. Spatial analysis of the second-leg manifest showed onward transport routing toward Turkey's eastern land border — in proximity to a heavily sanctioned region. Turkey is a friendly nation, but the route introduced transshipment exposure, an unverified forwarder, and proximity to an embargoed border: GR = 4.0.

Product & End-Use Risk

The engineering master data returned an active ECCN — 3A001.a.7.c, used here illustratively — for high-performance integrated circuits controlled for National Security (NS1) and Anti-Terrorism (AT1) reasons — a radiation-tolerant, military-temperature-grade variant with reprogrammable logic suited to guidance applications. (In practice a part of this class today would also be screened against the 3A090 / 4A090 advanced-computing controls of Chapter 5.3.) That places it in the Chapter 5 rubric's top row — a military-grade or radiation-hardened part — and the declared end-use of school drone kits was structurally inconsistent with both the part's capability and the buyer's profile. Both conditions the scoring engine requires are met: PR = 5.0.

10.3 The Computation

$$\mathbf{TRS = (w_1 \cdot ER) + (w_2 \cdot GR) + (w_3 \cdot PR)}$$
$$\mathbf{TRS = (0.40 \times 4.0) + (0.35 \times 4.0) + (0.25 \times 5.0)}$$
$$\mathbf{TRS = 1.60 + 1.40 + 1.25 = 4.25}$$

At 4.25, the order lands in the High-Risk tier. Note the effect of the weighting: even though only one pillar hit the maximum, the critical product signal (PR = 5) combined with the shell-entity signal (ER = 4) drove the score deep into the top band. An unweighted mean would have averaged the same inputs to a softer number and risked obscuring the threat.

There is a belt and suspenders here. The weighted score reaches High on its own — but the PR = 5 alone also trips the High floor, so even had the entity and route come in calm, this order could not have cleared. The aggregate and the floor agree, which is exactly what you want to see on a transaction like this one.

10.4 The Systemic Interlock

The instant the value resolved, the trigger executed the Chapter 6 High-Risk protocol, bypassing standard user permissions:

- **Database field lock.** Order state set to CRITICAL_BLOCK_LEGAL and the compliance lock flag flipped to TRUE, removing edit access from sales and account staff.
- **Physical inventory isolation.** The warehouse system segregated the 1,500 FPGAs from active stock and refused to generate picking tickets or packing slips.
- **Logistical manifest interlock.** The label engine blocked generation of air waybills, carrier labels, and customs declarations — the goods physically could not move.

10.5 The Investigation

With the order frozen, the file routed automatically to legal counsel and the Chief Compliance Officer for Enhanced Due Diligence. A deep ownership audit pierced the proxy directors on the invoice and mapped the share structure to an unlisted parent — ultimately tied to a defense-linked procurement entity operating on behalf of an end-user in a sanctioned region. The "school drone kit" story collapsed. The transaction was rejected and reported.

10.6 The Shield in Application

Two things protected the enterprise. First, the block itself — the goods never shipped. Second, and just as important, the record: a versioned, tamper-evident log showing the exact pillar scores, the weighted computation, the timestamp, the analyst, and the supporting documents. Had a regulator asked why this order was stopped and a hundred others cleared, the answer was a single reproducible number and the trail behind it.

10.7 Validation Script

```
weights = (0.40, 0.35, 0.25)
er, gr, pr = 4.0, 4.0, 5.0

trs = round(sum(w * s for w, s in zip(weights, (er, gr, pr))), 2)
print(f"TRS = {trs}")                    # 4.25
print("HIGH RISK - HARD STOP" if trs >= 3.9 else "REVIEW")
```

Reproducing SO-2026-88421 : the same inputs always yield the same score — the definition of a defensible methodology.

Epilogue: What Happened to SO-2026-88421

Return to Dana's desk, 4:50 p.m., quarter's end. In the old world she had a green CLEAR flag, a vague unease, and a clock. In the new one she has three rubrics and a formula. She grades the buyer a 4, the route a 4, the product a 5. The system does the arithmetic she used to do in her stomach: 4.25. High Risk. The screen does not offer her a button to release it. It offers her a case number.

The order she would have shipped on a Friday feeling never leaves the warehouse. The 1,500 FPGAs stay locked to the floor while counsel unwinds an ownership chain that ends somewhere it should never have been allowed to begin. The quarter closes a little lighter and the company stays exactly where it wants to be — off an enforcement docket.

That is the whole argument of this manual in one transaction. The Red Flags were always there; Dana saw every one of them. What she lacked was a way to convert what she saw into a number that could not be argued down, wired into a system that would act on it without her having to win a fight at 4:50 on a Friday. The framework does not replace the analyst's judgment. It gives that judgment a spine — and a memory that will still be standing, unbroken and time-stamped, on the day a regulator comes to read it.

Appendix A · Quick-Reference Scorecard

The three pillars, at a glance

Score	Entity (ER)	Geographic (GR)	Product (PR)
1	Public, established, verified owner	Direct to Tier-1 ally	EAR99 COTS item
2	Stable SME, transparent address	Friendly nation, logical layover	Industrial-grade, broad use
3	New (<2 yr), thin footprint	Transshipment hub + generic forwarder	Dual-use over threshold; vague R&D
4	Virtual office; address mismatch	Borders a sanctioned/embargoed state	Listed ECCN; license may apply
5	Shares site with listed party; EUS refusal	Circuitous; multiple unverified forwarders	Mil/rad-hardened; end-use mismatch

Formula and action bands

$$\mathbf{TRS = (0.40 \cdot ER) + (0.35 \cdot GR) + (0.25 \cdot PR)}$$

TRS range	Tier	Action
1.00 – 2.49	Low	Greenlight; standard DPS screening; archive score.
2.50 – 3.89	Medium	EDD hold; notarized EUS; facility verification; manager sign-off. Product-floor (PR = 4) holds route to a trade-compliance license determination.
3.90 – 5.00	High	Hard stop; block shipping; legal review or rejection; file suspicious-order report.

Single-pillar floors: any pillar scored 5 forces a minimum tier of High (hard stop); a Product pillar scored 4 (CCL-listed) forces a minimum tier of Medium (hold), so no listed item auto-clears — the same floor is recommended for

Entity 4 and Geographic 4. The aggregate may raise the tier but never lower it below what a single pillar demands.

Appendix B · Glossary & Regulatory References

BIS — Bureau of Industry and Security — the U.S. Department of Commerce agency that administers the EAR and the Commerce Control List.

CCL — Commerce Control List — the list of items subject to specific export controls, organized by ECCN.

COTS — Commercial off-the-shelf — standard commercial hardware not specially designed for military use.

DPS — Denied Parties Screening — automated name-matching against government watchlists.

Dual-use — An item with both civilian and potential military/proliferation applications.

EAR — Export Administration Regulations (15 CFR Parts 730–774) — the U.S. rules governing dual-use exports.

EAR99 — A designation for items subject to the EAR but not listed on the CCL; generally low-control.

ECCN — Export Control Classification Number — the alphanumeric code identifying a controlled item on the CCL (e.g., 3A001).

EDD — Enhanced Due Diligence — the elevated review triggered by a Medium-tier score.

EDI — Electronic Data Interchange — automated system-to-system exchange of purchase orders.

Entity List — A BIS list of parties subject to specific license requirements for reasons of national security or foreign policy.

EUS — End-User Statement — a signed declaration of the true end-user and end-use of the goods.

FPGA — Field-Programmable Gate Array — a reconfigurable integrated circuit; frequently dual-use.

SDN List — OFAC's Specially Designated Nationals list — sanctioned individuals and entities (administered separately from BIS).

Transshipment — Routing goods through an intermediate hub or country en route to the final destination.

TRS — Transaction Risk Score — the weighted 1.0–5.0 index at the center of this framework.

UBO — Ultimate Beneficial Owner — the natural person(s) who ultimately own or control an entity.

Key regulatory references

- 15 CFR Part 732 — Steps for using the EAR, including "Know Your Customer" guidance and Red Flags.
- 15 CFR Part 744 — Control policy: end-use and end-user based restrictions.
- 15 CFR Part 762 — Recordkeeping (minimum five-year retention).
- 15 CFR Part 774 — The Commerce Control List and ECCN definitions.

References are provided for orientation only and were current as of drafting; confirm the operative text of each provision before relying on it.